How to Overcome Depression Through Diet, Exercise, and Mindset Shifts

A Holistic Guide to Improving Your Mood and Mental Health

The Fix-It Guy

Table of Contents

Introduction

Welcome to a journey of transformation and triumph! If you've ever felt the weight of the world on your shoulders, battling the shadows of depression, you're not alone. I've been there too, navigating the stormy seas of mental health, desperately searching for a lifeline. But fear not, my friend, for this book isn't just a guide; it's your compass, your map, and your sturdy ship through those tempestuous waters.

In "How to Overcome Depression Through Diet, Exercise, and Mindset Shifts," we're not offering you a one-size-fits-all solution. No quick fixes or magic potions here. Instead, picture this as a personal conversation over a cup of warm tea or coffee, where we dive deep into the science, heart, and humor of rediscovering your joy.

Have you ever wondered, mid-bite of a chocolate bar or during a midnight stroll, if there's more to your cravings and wanderings than meets the eye? Spoiler alert: there is! We're about to embark on a quest to unravel the mysteries of your mind, decode the language of your gut, and unleash the potential of your body to be your ally in the battle against the blues.

But wait, there's more! We'll explore the invigorating world of exercise, not as a punishment for indulging in that extra slice of pizza but as a celebration of what your body can achieve. And brace yourself for mindset shifts that'll make Tony Stark's suit upgrades seem like child's play. Because, my friend, you're not just turning the pages; you're turning your life around.

Buckle up for laughter, tears, and aha moments as we navigate the tumultuous seas of self-discovery. This isn't just a book; it's your backstage pass to a life filled with vitality, resilience, and, dare I say it, a sprinkle of magic. Let's embark on this adventure together, shall we? Your brighter, bolder, and happier self awaits!

Chapter 1

Foundations of Mental Health

The Mind-Body Connection

Hey there, mental health explorer! Today, we're diving into the wild world of the mind-body connection. No lab coats or complex theories here, just a friendly chat about how what's going on in your noggin affects every inch of your fabulous self.

Step 1: Embrace the Unity of Mind and Body
Imagine your mind and body throwing a lively dance party, they're grooving together, and the playlist is your overall well-being. This connection isn't just philosophical mumbo-jumbo; it's the real deal. Your thoughts, feelings, and bodily sensations are like BFFs sharing secrets at a sleepover. Start by acknowledging this duo dynamic.

Troubleshooting: Feeling skeptical? That's cool! Sometimes, the mind-body connection seems as elusive as a cat video on the internet. But hey, take a deep breath and let it sink in. Trust me; they're in cahoots!

Step 2: Listen to Your Body's Whispers

Your body is like a chatterbox, always dropping hints about your mood. Notice how your shoulders tense up when stress pays a visit? Your body spills the beans before your brain even realizes it. Pay attention to those subtle signals; they're like the Morse code of your emotions.

Troubleshooting: If your body is speaking in riddles, fret not. Take a moment to check-in. Ask yourself, "What's the sensation? Where is it?" It's like decoding your body's secret language, and you're the Sherlock Holmes of your well-being.

Step 3: Nurture Your Mind, Nurture Your Body

Now, let's talk about TLC for your mental health. Just as your car needs regular oil changes, your mind needs some care too. Engage in activities that make your heart sing, be it doodling, dancing, or daydreaming. Your mind will thank you, and your body will join the celebration.

Troubleshooting: "But I don't have time for self-care!" I hear you. Start small. It could be a five-minute dance break or a deep-breathing moment. Your mind and body don't demand grand gestures; they appreciate the little things.

Step 4: Feed Your Mind with Positivity
Think of your mind as a garden. Nurture it with positivity, and watch those beautiful thoughts bloom. Surround yourself with uplifting people, indulge in laughter, and let go of negativity like yesterday's news. A happy mind sets the stage for a healthy body.

Troubleshooting: Negative thoughts barging in? Show them the exit. Challenge them with positive affirmations or distract your mind with something delightful. It's like telling those gloomy thoughts, "You're not on the guest list."

Key Takeaways:
- Your mind and body are the ultimate power duo.
- Listen to your body; it's dropping hints like a master detective.
- TLC for your mind equals TLC for your body.
- Feed your mind with positivity, and watch your world transform.

Next Steps:
Ready to rock this mind-body connection? Start by noticing one small sensation in your body today. Treat it with kindness, and observe how your mind responds. It's the first step on this groovy journey to better mental health. See you on the flip side!

Impact of Diet, Exercise, and Mindset on Mental Well-being

Diet, Exercise, and Mindset. Think of them as the Avengers of your well-being, each playing a unique role in the epic saga of your mental health.

Step 1: You Are What You Eat, Literally

Picture your brain as a gourmet chef. It needs the finest ingredients to whip up those neurotransmitters – the brain's secret sauce for mood regulation. Start by choosing foods rich in Omega-3 fatty acids, like fish, nuts, and seeds. These are your brain's version of superhero fuel.

Troubleshooting: "But chocolate is my soul food!" Fear not, my friend. Dark chocolate, in moderation, can be your ally. It's like a tiny superhero cape for your taste buds.

Step 2: Hydration – The Aquaman of Mental Wellness

Water, the unsung hero! Dehydration can play tricks on your mind, making you feel sluggish and irritable. So, gulp down that H2O and let Aquaman keep your mental seas calm.

Troubleshooting: Forgetful about water? Set a quirky reminder, like naming your water bottle "Hydration Station." Quirky, but it works!

Step 3: Sweat Out the Stress

Enter the arena of exercise, where stress meets its match. You don't need to run a marathon; a brisk walk or a dance party in your living room will do. Exercise releases endorphins, your body's very own mood elevators.

Troubleshooting: "I'm too busy to exercise!" We've all been there. Sneak it into your routine; take the stairs, do squats while waiting for your coffee. Exercise doesn't need an invitation; it can join the party anytime!

Step 4: Find Your Exercise Soulmate

Exercise isn't a punishment; it's a celebration of what your body can do. Pick activities you love, whether it's yoga, cycling, or interpretive dance. Your mindset about exercise makes all the difference.

Troubleshooting: Hate the gym? No problemo. Nature is a free gym membership. Take a hike, literally!

Step 5: Rewire Your Brain with Positivity

Your mindset is like the director's cut of your life's movie. Choose the positive scenes, and cut out the negativity. Practice gratitude, challenge negative thoughts, and surround yourself with uplifting vibes.

Troubleshooting: "Negativity follows me like a shadow!" Shine a light on it. Create a gratitude journal; it's like a spotlight for the good stuff.

Step 6: Mindfulness – The Jedi Mind Trick
Ever wished you could hit pause on life's chaos? Mindfulness is your Jedi mind trick. Whether through meditation, deep breathing, or simply savoring a moment, it's your ticket to mental clarity.

Troubleshooting: "My mind won't shut up!" It's okay; minds are chatty. Start with small doses. Even a few minutes of mindful breathing can silence the mind's chatter.

Key Takeaways:
- Nutrition fuels your brain – choose your meals wisely.
- Exercise is a celebration, not a chore.
- Your mindset directs the blockbuster of your life.

Next Steps:
Ready for action? Choose one small diet tweak, incorporate a mini-exercise routine, or start a daily gratitude practice. Your mental Avengers are gearing up for an epic battle against the blues. Join the squad!

Chapter 2

Nourishing Your Body and Mind

Nutrition and its Role in Mental Health

Greetings, health enthusiasts! Today, we're diving into the world of nutrition, where every bite is like a brushstroke on the canvas of your mental well-being. Picture this chapter as a culinary adventure – we're not just feeding your body; we're feeding your mind, one delicious revelation at a time.

Step 1: Food as Fuel for Thought
Your brain is a powerhouse, and it needs the right nutrients to function at its peak. It's not about counting calories; it's about quality. Imagine your brain doing a happy dance when you treat it to nutrient-rich foods like fruits, veggies, whole grains, and lean proteins.

Troubleshooting: "But burgers are my love language!" No worries! Opt for leaner meats, or venture into the world of veggie burgers. Your taste buds won't know what hit them!

Step 2: Omega-3 Fatty Acids – The Brain's BFF

Meet the brain's best friend, Omega-3 fatty acids. Found in fish, flaxseeds, and walnuts, these little wonders are like a spa day for your brain cells. They enhance mood, boost focus, and make your brain feel like a million bucks.

Troubleshooting: "I'm not a fish person!" No need to swim with the fish. Try chia seeds or flaxseed oil for a plant-based omega-3 boost.

Step 3: Water – The Elixir of Mental Clarity

Let's talk about the unsung hero of mental well-being – water. Dehydration can turn your brain into a desert, leaving you parched and cranky. Aim for those eight glasses a day, and watch your mental fog lift.

Troubleshooting: "I forget to drink water!" Make it a game. Every time you check your phone, take a sip. Your hydration app just got an upgrade!

Step 4: Mindful Eating – Savor the Flavor

Eating isn't a race; it's a journey. Practice mindful eating, savor each bite, appreciate the flavors, and listen to your body's cues. It's like a meditation session for your taste buds.

Troubleshooting: "I inhale my food!" Slow down, Speedy Gonzales. Put your fork down between bites, chew thoroughly, and enjoy the symphony of flavors.

Step 5: Probiotics – Happy Belly, Happy Mind
Ever felt "butterflies in your stomach" before a big moment? Your gut and brain are in constant communication. Probiotics, found in yogurt, kefir, and fermented foods, keep your gut flora happy, influencing your mood and stress levels.

Troubleshooting: "I'm lactose intolerant!" No worries; there are dairy-free probiotic options like sauerkraut and kimchi. Your gut party is still on!

Key Takeaways:
- Your brain needs quality nutrients, not just calories.
- Omega-3 fatty acids are the brain's besties.
- Water is the unsung hero of mental clarity.
- Mindful eating is a meditation for your taste buds.
- Probiotics keep your gut and brain in sync.

Next Steps:

Ready to upgrade your menu for mental bliss? Start small, add a handful of berries to your breakfast, swap that soda for water, or savor a meal without distractions. Your body and mind are about to embark on a gastronomic adventure. Bon appétit!

Superfoods for Mood Enhancement

Get ready to embark on a culinary journey that will have your taste buds doing the cha-cha and your mood doing a happy tango. We're talking about superfoods – the caped crusaders of the culinary world, here to elevate your mood to superhero status.

Dark Chocolate – The Dessert Avenger:
If there ever was a dessert with superpowers, it's dark chocolate. Packed with antioxidants and a dash of serotonin, this cocoa delight is more than just a guilty pleasure, it's a mood-boosting ninja. Grab a piece and let the endorphins party!

Troubleshooting: "But milk chocolate is my go-to!" Fear not, sweet tooth! Opt for dark chocolate with lower sugar content, and you'll still get the mood-lifting benefits.

Berries – The Colorful Sidekicks:
Meet the vibrant sidekicks of the superfood squad – berries. Blueberries, strawberries, and raspberries are bursting with antioxidants and vitamin C, working together to combat stress and boost your immune system. They're like a fruity symphony for your mood.

Troubleshooting: "Fresh berries are expensive!" No worries, frozen berries are just as nutrient-packed. Toss them into your smoothie or sprinkle them on yogurt for a mood-boosting feast.

Nuts and Seeds – The Snack Avengers:
Craving a crunchy snack? Nuts and seeds are your go-to Avengers. Almonds, walnuts, chia seeds, and flaxseeds are rich in omega-3 fatty acids and magnesium, promoting brain health and reducing stress. It's like a power-packed snack attack!

Troubleshooting: "I'm allergic to nuts!" Seeds to the rescue! Sunflower seeds, pumpkin seeds, and chia seeds are nut-free alternatives that still bring mood-boosting magic.

Fatty Fish – The Oceanic Marvel:
Dive into the oceanic marvel of fatty fish like salmon, mackerel, and trout. Loaded with omega-3 fatty acids, these aquatic heroes support brain function, reduce inflammation, and give your mood a refreshing swim in the positive vibes.

Troubleshooting: "I don't like the fishy taste!" Give it a flavorful twist. Marinate your fish with herbs and spices or grill it with a squeeze of citrus to make it a taste sensation.

Avocado – The Creamy Crusader:

Avocado, the creamy crusader, is not just Instagram-worthy; it's a mood-enhancing powerhouse. Packed with healthy fats, vitamins, and potassium, avocados provide sustained energy and keep your mood soaring high.

Troubleshooting: "Avocado is too expensive!" It's an investment in your mood! Look for sales or buy in bulk, your taste buds and brain will thank you.

Key Takeaways:
- Dark chocolate is a mood-boosting ninja.
- Berries are the vibrant sidekicks combating stress.
- Nuts and seeds are the crunchy snack Avengers.
- Fatty fish swim in omega-3 goodness for brain health.
- Avocado is the creamy crusader for sustained energy.

Next Steps:

Ready to assemble your superfood squad? Add a handful of berries to your breakfast, snack on nuts, indulge in dark chocolate, or make a delicious avocado toast. Your mood is about to be on the superhero level, cape optional!

The Gut-Brain Connection

Greetings, fellow explorers of the mind-gut galaxy! Today, we're embarking on a journey through the intricate network that links our gut and brain – a connection so profound, it's like a symphony where every note influences the melody of our well-being.

Step 1: The Cosmic Communication

Picture your gut and brain as pen pals, constantly sending messages to each other. This two-way street, known as the gut-brain axis, is a superhighway of chemical signals, influencing not only your digestion but also your mood, emotions, and overall mental health.

Troubleshooting: "I don't feel any connection!" Fear not, cosmic traveler. It's subtle, like a gentle breeze. Begin by tuning in to your gut feelings, literally and metaphorically.

Step 2: Gut Microbes – The Galactic Gardeners

Within your gut resides a bustling metropolis of microbes, the microbiota. Think of them as tiny gardeners tending to the landscape of your well-being. These microbes produce neurotransmitters, the brain's messengers, influencing your mood and emotions.

Troubleshooting: "Microbes in my gut? Sounds creepy!" It's a bustling community! Embrace it by incorporating probiotics and fermented foods into your diet. It's like inviting friendly neighbors to the cosmic block party.

Step 3: Serotonin – The Mood Maestro

Meet serotonin, the mood maestro produced in both your gut and brain. It regulates mood, appetite, and sleep. A happy gut equals a happy brain, and vice versa. Foods rich in tryptophan, like turkey, eggs, and nuts, contribute to serotonin production.

Troubleshooting: "I'm always in a bad mood!" Let's boost that serotonin production. Add tryptophan-rich foods to your diet, and watch the mood maestro conduct a happier symphony.

Step 4: Stress, Digestion, and Harmony

Stress is the disruptor of this cosmic harmony. When stress hits, it can throw the gut-brain axis out of sync, affecting digestion and triggering mood swings. Techniques like deep breathing, meditation, and yoga act as cosmic balancers, restoring the equilibrium.

Troubleshooting: "I'm too stressed to meditate!" Start small, like a micro-meditation. Focus on your breath for just a few minutes; it's like a mini spa break for your mind and gut.

Step 5: Nourishing the Cosmic Connection

Your diet plays a pivotal role in maintaining this cosmic connection. High-fiber foods, like fruits, veggies, and whole grains, act as fuel for your gut microbes. A well-nourished gut creates a harmonious environment for your brain to thrive.

Troubleshooting: "I'm not a fan of veggies!" Mix it up. Sneak veggies into smoothies, experiment with different recipes, and let your taste buds explore the cosmic menu.

Key Takeaways:
- The gut and brain communicate through the gut-brain axis.
- Gut microbes influence mood and emotions.
- Serotonin, produced in the gut, regulates mood.
- Stress disrupts the cosmic harmony, balance is key.
- A nourished gut supports overall mental well-being.

Next Steps:

Ready to nourish your cosmic connection? Add fiber-rich foods to your plate, try a stress-balancing activity, or embark on a gut-friendly culinary adventure.

Your gut and brain are ready to dance to the rhythm of well-being!

Chapter 3

Exercise as a Pillar of Mental Wellness

Benefits of Physical Activity for Mental Health

Hello, champions of mental well-being! Today, we're lacing up our metaphorical sneakers and diving into the exhilarating world of exercise, the unsung hero in the epic saga of mental wellness. Think of this chapter as your trainer for the mind, guiding you through the countless perks that a good workout brings to your mental health.

Step 1: Endorphin Explosion

Ever heard of the "runner's high"? It's not just for marathoners. Exercise releases endorphins, your body's natural mood lifters. It's like a burst of joy, a euphoric symphony that plays in the background as you move and groove.

Troubleshooting: "I hate running!" No worries, friend. Dance, swim, cycle, choose an activity that makes you smile. The endorphin party doesn't discriminate.

Step 2: Stress-Busting Sweat Session

Stressed out? Enter the stress-busting superhero, exercise. Whether it's a brisk walk or an intense workout, physical activity reduces stress hormones and triggers the release of chemicals that enhance your mood.

Troubleshooting: "I'm too busy for a workout!" Sneak it in. Take short breaks for stretching or a quick walk. It's like a power nap for your brain.

Step 3: Boosted Brainpower

Exercise isn't just a workout for your muscles; it's a workout for your brain. It enhances cognitive function, sharpens focus, and improves memory. It's like giving your brain a superhero cape, ready to tackle mental challenges.

Troubleshooting: "I'm not a gym person!" No need for a membership. Take the stairs, have a dance break, or go for a hike, make it fun, and your brain will thank you.

Step 4: Anxiety Armor

Ever notice that after a good workout, your worries seem to shrink? Exercise is like armor against anxiety. It reduces the intensity of anxious feelings and provides a shield of calmness.

Troubleshooting: "I feel too anxious to exercise!" Start slow. Yoga or gentle walks are fantastic anxiety allies. The goal is progress, not perfection.

Step 5: Sleep Serenity

Struggling with sleep? Exercise is your ticket to the land of nod. It improves sleep quality, helping you drift into a deeper, more restorative slumber.

Troubleshooting: "I'm too tired to exercise!" Paradoxical, right? A short, gentle workout can boost energy levels and promote better sleep. It's like a magic wand for bedtime.

Key Takeaways:

- Exercise releases endorphins for a natural mood lift.
- Physical activity is a stress-busting superhero.
- It boosts brainpower and enhances cognitive function.
- Exercise acts as armor against anxiety.
- Improved sleep quality is a bonus benefit.

Next Steps:

Ready to unleash the mental wellness superhero within you? Start with a 10-minute activity you enjoy, whether it's a dance, a brisk walk, or a quick workout routine. Your mind and body are about to experience the superhero transformation, one move at a time!

Finding the Right Exercise Routine

Hey there, fitness explorer! Choosing the right exercise routine is like finding the perfect dance partner, it should match your rhythm, make you feel alive, and leave you wanting more. In this chapter, we're on a quest to discover the workout routine that aligns with your preferences, goals, and, most importantly, your enjoyment.

Step 1: Know Thyself
Before diving into the world of fitness, take a moment to reflect on your preferences and goals. Are you a solo warrior or a group adventurer? Do you crave the zen of yoga or the intensity of high-intensity workouts? Knowing yourself is the compass guiding you to the right exercise haven.

Troubleshooting: "I have no idea where to start!" No worries, friend. Start with what you enjoy. If you love dancing, explore dance workouts. If nature beckons, consider hiking or cycling. The journey is about joy, not judgment.

Step 2: Mix It Up
Variety is the spice of fitness life. Experiment with different types of exercises to keep things interesting. From cardio to strength training to flexibility exercises,

your body and mind benefit from a diverse workout routine. It's like having a fitness buffet where every dish serves a purpose.

Troubleshooting: "I get bored easily!" Join the club! Mix up your routine weekly. Try a new class, discover a new trail, or incorporate different exercises into your regimen. Your routine should be as dynamic as you are.

Step 3: Set Realistic Goals

Goals are the North Star guiding your fitness journey. Set realistic, achievable goals that excite you. Whether it's mastering a new yoga pose, running a certain distance, or simply feeling more energized, these goals will be your milestones, marking your progress.

Troubleshooting: "I'm overwhelmed by the big goals!" Break them down. Instead of aiming for a marathon, start with a 5K. Small victories lead to significant triumphs. Celebrate each milestone on your path.

Step 4: Consistency Trumps Intensity

Consistency is the superhero of fitness. It's not about crushing it in one intense session; it's about regular, sustainable activity. Find a routine that fits your schedule and becomes a natural part of your day. It's like creating a habit that your future self will thank you for.

Troubleshooting: "I can't stick to a routine!" Simplify. Start with short sessions, gradually increasing duration. Consistency is about showing up, even on days when the sofa calls your name.

Step 5: Listen to Your Body
Your body is the best fitness coach. Listen to its signals. If a certain exercise causes discomfort, modify or choose an alternative. It's like having a workout buddy who knows when to push and when to ease off.

Troubleshooting: "I'm not sure if I'm doing it right!" Seek guidance. Whether it's a fitness app, a trainer, or a friend, having a support system ensures you're on the right track. Form matters, but so does having fun.

Key Takeaways:
- Know your preferences and goals.
- Embrace variety for a well-rounded routine.
- Set realistic and exciting fitness goals.
- Consistency beats intensity for long-term success.
- Listen to your body and adjust as needed.

Next Steps:
Ready to dance with your fitness routine? Experiment with different activities, set achievable goals, and make

consistency your fitness mantra. The right routine is out there, waiting for you to discover the joy of movement!

Incorporating Movement into Daily Life

Ahoy, daily life navigators! In this chapter, we're transforming the mundane into the magnificent by weaving movement seamlessly into the fabric of your everyday routine. No need for fancy equipment or structured workouts, we're talking about embracing the joy of movement in the most ordinary moments.

Step 1: The Morning Ritual Dance

Rise and shine, sleepyhead! Kick off your day with a burst of movement. Whether it's a brief stretching routine, a few yoga poses, or even a spontaneous dance to your favorite song, let your morning set the tone for an energetic day.

Troubleshooting: "I'm not a morning person!" No worries. Start with gentle stretches in bed or a quick stroll around your space. It's about waking up your body, not necessarily the crack of dawn.

Step 2: The Desk Dose of Energy

Desk-bound? No problem! Break the shackles of sedentary life with micro-movements. Stretch your arms, rotate your ankles, or do seated leg lifts. These mini exercises keep your blood flowing and energy levels up.

Troubleshooting: "I have a tight schedule!" Sneak in short bursts. Set an hourly alarm to stand, stretch, or take a quick walk. It's like hitting the reset button for your mind and body.

Step 3: Walk, Don't Scroll

Turn your scrolling habit into a stroll habit. Instead of mindlessly scrolling through your phone, take a stroll around your neighborhood or office. It's a simple way to inject movement into your day while giving your eyes a break.

Troubleshooting: "I'm glued to my phone!" Make it a habit. Set a daily goal for steps or designate phone-free zones where movement takes center stage. Your steps can be as small as your commitment.

Step 4: TV Time Turnaround

Love binge-watching your favorite shows? Make it an active affair. During TV time, incorporate stretches, bodyweight exercises, or even pedal on a stationary bike. It's like a workout that comes with a side of entertainment.

Troubleshooting: "I just want to relax!" Multi-task relaxation. You can stretch or do yoga poses while catching up on your favorite series. It's relaxation with a twist.

Step 5: Family/Friend Fitness Fiesta
Turn socializing into a movement extravaganza. Instead of meeting for coffee, opt for a walk-and-talk session. Invite friends or family for a friendly sports match or dance party. It's like combining quality time with fitness fun.

Troubleshooting: "My friends aren't into fitness!" Be the trendsetter. Propose new, active activities, and you might just inspire your circle to join the movement revolution.

Key Takeaways:
- Start your day with a burst of morning movement.
- Incorporate micro-movements at your desk.
- Turn scrolling time into a walking habit.
- Make TV time an opportunity for active exercises.
- Transform socializing into a fitness fiesta.

Next Steps:
Ready to sprinkle movement throughout your day? Choose one or two steps from above and experiment with incorporating them into your routine. Movement isn't a separate task; it's a vibrant thread woven into the tapestry of your daily life!

Chapter 4

Mindset Shifts for a Positive Outlook

Cognitive Behavioral Strategies

Greetings, mindset architects! In this chapter, we're delving into the art of sculpting your mental landscape, turning it into a masterpiece of positivity. Say goodbye to the gloomy clouds and hello to the sunshine as we explore cognitive-behavioral strategies to foster a resilient and optimistic mindset.

Step 1: Embrace the Power of Positive Self-Talk

Your mind is an echo chamber, and what you tell yourself matters. Swap the negative soundtrack for a positive jam. When faced with challenges, replace self-defeating thoughts with encouraging ones. It's like being your own motivational speaker.

Troubleshooting: "I'm not good at positive affirmations!" Start small. Acknowledge one positive thing about yourself each day. It could be as simple as recognizing your effort or resilience.

Step 2: Challenge Negative Thoughts

Imagine negative thoughts as uninvited guests crashing your mental party. Challenge them! Ask yourself if they're based on facts or assumptions. It's like being a detective, separating fact from fiction in the case of your own mindset.

Troubleshooting: "Negative thoughts are relentless!" Counteract them with evidence. If your mind says, "I can't do this," remind yourself of past achievements or times you overcame similar challenges.

Step 3: Reframe Problems into Opportunities

Life throws curveballs, but what if you see them as opportunities for growth? Reframe problems into challenges to conquer. It's like turning roadblocks into stepping stones on your journey to a positive mindset.

Troubleshooting: "Every problem feels like a mountain!" Break it down. Instead of seeing the whole mountain, focus on the next step. Progress, no matter how small, is still a move forward.

Step 4: Practice Gratitude Daily

Gratitude is the secret sauce for a positive outlook. Each day, jot down three things you're grateful for. It's like planting seeds of positivity that grow into a garden of resilience.

Troubleshooting: "I forget to practice gratitude!" Set a reminder, or link it to a daily habit like your morning coffee. Soon, gratitude will become as routine as brushing your teeth.

Step 5: Cultivate a Growth Mindset

Imagine your mind as a garden where thoughts bloom. Cultivate a growth mindset by embracing challenges as opportunities to learn and grow. It's like planting seeds of curiosity, resilience, and a love for continuous improvement.

Troubleshooting: "I fear failure!" Redefine failure as a stepping stone to success. Ask yourself, "What can I learn from this?" It's a mindset shift from defeat to discovery.

Key Takeaways:
- Harness the power of positive self-talk.
- Challenge and reframe negative thoughts.
- See problems as opportunities for growth.
- Practice gratitude daily for a resilient mindset.
- Cultivate a growth mindset for continuous improvement.

Next Steps:
Ready to sculpt your mental masterpiece? Pick one strategy that resonates with you and incorporate it into

your daily routine. Over time, these mindset shifts will shape a brighter, more positive outlook on life. Onward to positivity!

Cultivating a Growth Mindset

Greetings, fellow cultivators of mental landscapes! In this chapter, we embark on a journey to transform our minds into fertile gardens where the seeds of curiosity, resilience, and continuous growth flourish. Brace yourselves as we explore the art of cultivating a growth mindset, a mindset that sees challenges as opportunities and embraces the journey of lifelong learning.

Step 1: Embrace Challenges as Opportunities

In the garden of the mind, challenges are not weeds; they are the seeds of growth. Rather than fearing difficulties, see them as stepping stones to new heights. It's like a gardener eagerly anticipating the first signs of a sprout breaking through the soil.

Troubleshooting: "Challenges feel overwhelming!" Break them down into smaller tasks. Tackle one aspect at a time, like tending to individual plants in your mental garden. Progress is progress, no matter how incremental.

Step 2: Learn from Criticism

Picture criticism as the rain that nurtures your mental garden. Instead of seeing it as a downpour, view it as a vital source of growth. Extract lessons, adapt, and let the feedback contribute to the flourishing landscape of your mindset.

Troubleshooting: "Criticism feels like a storm!" Separate the constructive from the destructive. Consider the feedback objectively, like evaluating the soil quality in your garden. Use what nourishes, and discard what doesn't.

Step 3: Embrace the Power of Yet

Add the magical word "yet" to your vocabulary. If you catch yourself saying, "I can't do this," transform it into "I can't do this yet." It's like planting a seed of potential that will blossom with time and effort.

Troubleshooting: "I feel stuck!" Shift your focus. Instead of fixating on what you can't do, celebrate what you can do. It's like appreciating the growth of each individual plant in your garden, acknowledging progress.

Step 4: View Effort as the Path to Mastery

In the garden of a growth mindset, effort is the sunlight that fuels growth. See each endeavor, whether successful or not, as a valuable experience on the path to mastery. It's like enjoying the process of nurturing your mental garden, appreciating the journey.

Troubleshooting: "I feel discouraged!" Celebrate effort, not just outcomes. Acknowledge the time and energy invested, similar to tending to the soil before witnessing the bloom. Progress is a reward in itself.

Step 5: Surround Yourself with Growth-Minded Individuals

In the communal garden of growth mindsets, each member contributes to the collective growth. Surround yourself with individuals who share this mindset, fostering an environment where learning and improvement are celebrated.

Troubleshooting: "My environment doesn't support growth!" Plant seeds of change. Engage in conversations about growth and learning. Like introducing new plant species to your garden, gradually transform your mental landscape.

Key Takeaways:
- Embrace challenges as opportunities for growth.
- Learn from criticism to nourish your mindset.
- Add "yet" to your vocabulary for potential.
- View effort as the path to mastery.
- Surround yourself with growth-minded individuals.

Next Steps:
Ready to cultivate a growth mindset garden? Start with one step, perhaps embracing a challenge or viewing effort as a path to mastery. Your mental garden is ready to bloom with the richness of continuous learning and growth!

Mindfulness and Meditation Practices

Welcome, seekers of tranquility and clarity! In this chapter, we'll embark on a serene exploration into the realms of mindfulness and meditation, powerful practices that anchor you in the present moment and provide a sanctuary for your mind to find peace.

Step 1: Understanding Mindfulness

Imagine a mental state where your attention is fully immersed in the present moment, free from the pull of the past or the tug of the future. That's mindfulness. It's like becoming the observer of your thoughts, acknowledging them without judgment.

Troubleshooting: "My mind wanders a lot!" Gently guide it back. When your thoughts meander, redirect your focus to the present, your breath, sensations, or the sounds around you. It's a mental nudge, not a scolding.

Step 2: The Art of Mindful Breathing

Your breath is a timeless anchor to the present. Engage in mindful breathing by focusing your attention on the inhale and exhale. It's like riding the gentle waves of your breath, allowing them to carry you to a calmer mental shore.

Troubleshooting: "I feel restless!" Embrace the rhythm. Start with short sessions and gradually extend them. Feel the rise and fall of your breath, letting it guide you into a state of tranquility.

Step 3: Exploring Guided Meditations
Guided meditations are like a soothing voice guiding you through a mental landscape. Whether it's a guided body scan, loving-kindness meditation, or a visualization journey, let the words be your companions on the path to serenity.

Troubleshooting: "My mind is too busy!" Appreciate the guidance. Guided meditations offer a focal point. Follow the instructions, allowing the words to create a mindful space amidst the mental chatter.

Step 4: Practicing Mindful Walking
Take your mindfulness on the move with mindful walking. Feel each step, notice the sensations in your body, and embrace the rhythm of your movement. It's like a dance with the present moment, where each step is a note in the melody of mindfulness.

Troubleshooting: "I'm always in a hurry!" Slow down. Even a brief mindful walk around your space can be transformative. Feel the ground beneath you and the air around you, savoring the act of walking.

Step 5: Finding Stillness in Meditation
Meditation is not a battle against thoughts; it's a journey into stillness. Find a comfortable seat, close your eyes, and focus on your breath or a chosen point of attention. It's like entering a serene sanctuary within, where the chaos of the mind gradually settles.

Troubleshooting: "I don't have time!" Start small. A few minutes of meditation can yield profound benefits. Set aside a dedicated time each day, and let it be a gift to your mental well-being.

Key Takeaways:
- Mindfulness is immersion in the present moment.
- Practice mindful breathing for mental grounding.
- Explore guided meditations for guided mental journeys.
- Incorporate mindful walking into your daily routine.
- Find stillness in meditation for inner tranquility.

Next Steps:
Ready to embark on your mindfulness and meditation journey? Choose one practice to start with, perhaps mindful breathing or a short guided meditation. Your mind is an oasis; these practices are the keys to unlock its serenity.

Chapter 5

Creating a Supportive Environment

Building a Strong Social Support Network

Hello, architects of positive connections! In this chapter, we're diving into the vital art of cultivating a supportive environment, a sanctuary where the seeds of well-being can flourish. Let's explore the importance of building a robust social support network to weather life's storms and celebrate its sunny days together.

Step 1: Recognizing the Power of Social Support
Imagine your support network as the pillars holding up the structure of your mental well-being. Social support is not just a luxury; it's a necessity. It's like having a safety net, a group of allies who stand by you through thick and thin.

Troubleshooting: "I'm a lone wolf!" Start small. Identify even one person – a friend, family member, or colleague, with whom you can share thoughts and feelings. It's like planting the first seed in your support garden.

Step 2: Quality Over Quantity

In the garden of relationships, it's the quality of connections that nurtures growth. Cultivate meaningful, genuine connections where you can be your authentic self. It's like tending to a garden with careful attention to each unique bloom.

Troubleshooting: "I have a lot of acquaintances but no close friends!" Nurture connections. Invest time and effort in those who reciprocate, creating a foundation of trust and understanding.

Step 3: Diversifying Your Support Ecosystem

Imagine your support network as a diverse ecosystem, with each member contributing in a unique way. Have friends, family, colleagues, and mentors. It's like planting various crops in your mental garden, ensuring a rich and varied harvest.

Troubleshooting: "I rely too much on one person!" Broaden your circle. Distribute the load, so no one person feels overwhelmed. It's like having different tools for different tasks in your support toolkit.

Step 4: Effective Communication

Communication is the water that nourishes the roots of your support network. Be open, honest, and clear about your needs. It's like watering your garden, consistent and transparent communication keeps your connections vibrant and healthy.

Troubleshooting: "I find it hard to express my feelings!" Practice vulnerability. Start with small, genuine shares and gradually build up. Your support network is there to listen and understand.

Step 5: Reciprocal Support

Imagine your support network as a garden where everyone contributes and benefits. Be willing to offer support as much as you receive. It's like a communal garden where each member tends to the well-being of others.

Troubleshooting: "I feel guilty asking for help!" Release the guilt. Just as you offer support, others find fulfillment in helping you. It's a shared journey, and everyone plays a role in the garden of support.

Key Takeaways:
- Social support is essential for mental well-being.
- Prioritize quality over quantity in relationships.

- Diversify your support network for a well-rounded ecosystem.
- Communicate openly about your needs and feelings.
- Reciprocal support creates a thriving support network.

Next Steps:
Ready to cultivate a supportive environment? Reflect on your current connections, identify areas for growth, and take small steps to nurture your social support network. Your mental garden is about to bloom with the vibrant colors of meaningful relationships!

Seeking Professional Help When Needed

Greetings, advocates for mental health! In this chapter, we're addressing a crucial aspect of well-being, the recognition that sometimes, the journey to mental wellness benefits from the guidance of a professional navigator. Let's explore the importance of seeking professional help when needed and how it can be a transformative step toward a healthier mind.

Step 1: Normalizing the Need for Professional Support
Imagine seeking professional help as consulting a skilled guide on a complex terrain. Just as you'd seek an expert for a physical ailment, your mental health deserves the same consideration. It's like acknowledging that professionals are trained allies in the quest for well-being.

Troubleshooting: "I fear judgment!" Release the stigma. Seeking help is a sign of strength, not weakness. Professionals are here to support without judgment, offering expertise to guide you on your unique journey.

Step 2: Recognizing the Signs
In the landscape of mental health, recognizing signs that indicate professional support is needed is crucial. Persistent feelings of sadness, overwhelming anxiety,

sleep disturbances, or difficulty managing daily activities may signal the need for expert guidance. It's like realizing you might need a map when the terrain becomes challenging.

Troubleshooting: "I'm not sure if it's serious enough!" Err on the side of caution. If your well-being feels compromised, seeking professional help is valid. A mental health professional can assess your situation and provide guidance.

Step 3: Understanding the Range of Professionals

Just as there are different specialists for various physical ailments, the mental health field boasts a diverse range of professionals. Psychologists, psychiatrists, therapists, counselors, each plays a unique role. It's like assembling a team of experts tailored to your specific needs.

Troubleshooting: "I don't know who to reach out to!" Start with a general practitioner or a mental health helpline. They can guide you to the appropriate professional based on your concerns. It's the first step in building your support team.

Step 4: Overcoming Barriers to Seeking Help

Barriers to seeking help are like roadblocks on the path to well-being. These can include financial concerns, stigma, or fear of the unknown. Recognize these barriers and explore solutions. Many professionals offer sliding scale fees, and online resources provide accessible information.

Troubleshooting: "I can't afford it!" Explore options. Many mental health professionals offer affordable services or operate on a sliding scale. Online platforms and helplines may also provide free resources. Your mental health is a priority worth investing in.

Step 5: Committing to the Process

Embarking on a journey with a mental health professional is a commitment to your well-being. It's like having a guide on a trek, consistency, honesty, and active participation in the process lead to meaningful progress.

Troubleshooting: "I feel overwhelmed!" Break it down. Professionals are there to guide you step by step. Each session is a manageable segment of your mental health journey. Trust the process, and embrace the support.

Key Takeaways:
- Normalize seeking professional help for mental health.
- Recognize signs indicating the need for expert guidance.
- Understand the range of mental health professionals.

- Overcome barriers to seeking help, including stigma.
- Commit to the process for meaningful progress.

Next Steps:
Ready to prioritize your mental well-being? If you recognize signs indicating the need for professional support, take the first step – whether it's reaching out to a general practitioner, seeking recommendations, or exploring online resources. Your mental health journey is unique, and professional guidance is a valuable companion on the path to well-being.

The Role of Positive Relationships in Mental Health

Greetings, champions of meaningful connections! In this exploration, we'll dive into the profound impact that positive relationships can have on mental health. Picture your relationships as the threads weaving the intricate tapestry of your well-being, each connection contributing to the vibrant colors of a fulfilling and balanced life.

Step 1: Social Support as a Pillar of Resilience
Imagine positive relationships as the bedrock of your mental fortress. Social support, characterized by trust, empathy, and understanding, acts as a shield against the storms of life. It's like having a support network that reinforces your mental well-being during challenging times.

Troubleshooting: "I'm not good at asking for help!" Start small. Share your thoughts and feelings with someone you trust. Vulnerability is the cornerstone of authentic connections.

Step 2: Emotional Validation and Understanding
In the landscape of positive relationships, emotional validation is the fertile soil where understanding blossoms. Feeling heard and understood nurtures

emotional well-being. It's like having a safe space where your emotions are acknowledged and accepted.

Troubleshooting: "I fear being judged!" Seek open-minded allies. Positive relationships are founded on acceptance and empathy. Surround yourself with individuals who appreciate your uniqueness.

Step 3: Celebrating Shared Moments

Positive relationships are not just about weathering storms; they're also about dancing in the sunshine. Celebrate shared joys and victories with loved ones. It's like creating a gallery of happy memories that you can revisit during challenging times.

Troubleshooting: "I don't have anyone to celebrate with!" Expand your circle. Engage in group activities, join clubs, or participate in community events. Shared interests are bridges to positive connections.

Step 4: Navigating Challenges Together

In the garden of positive relationships, challenges are not thorns but opportunities for growth. Facing difficulties alongside supportive individuals fosters resilience and mutual growth. It's like having companions on the journey, sharing the load and multiplying the strength.

Troubleshooting: "I tend to isolate myself during tough times!" Reach out. Positive relationships thrive on shared vulnerabilities. Allow others to support you, and let challenges become stepping stones to deeper connections.

Step 5: Setting Healthy Boundaries

Positive relationships flourish in an environment of respect and mutual understanding. Setting and respecting healthy boundaries ensures that connections remain supportive without becoming overwhelming. It's like tending to the garden of relationships, allowing each plant to thrive without overshadowing the others.

Troubleshooting: "I struggle with saying no!" Practice assertiveness. Communicate your needs clearly and respectfully. Positive relationships honor individual boundaries, creating a space where everyone can flourish.

Key Takeaways:

- Social support is a foundational pillar of mental resilience.
- Emotional validation fosters a sense of understanding and acceptance.
- Celebrating shared moments creates a treasury of positive memories.

- Navigating challenges together strengthens relationships and individuals.
- Setting healthy boundaries ensures balanced and supportive connections.

Next Steps:

Ready to enrich your mental landscape through positive relationships? Take a moment to reflect on your current connections, nurture existing bonds, and explore opportunities to forge new, positive relationships. Your mental well-being is intricately woven into the tapestry of meaningful connections!

Chapter 6

Overcoming Challenges and Setbacks

Resilience Building Techniques

Greetings, resilience warriors! In this chapter, we'll embark on a journey to fortify your mental fortress, arming you with techniques to bounce back from life's challenges and setbacks. Think of resilience as your superpower, and let's explore the tools that will make you an indomitable force in the face of adversity.

Step 1: Embracing the Power of Perspective

Imagine resilience as the lens through which you view challenges. Instead of seeing setbacks as insurmountable mountains, consider them as opportunities for growth. It's like adjusting the focus on a camera – zoom out to see the broader picture and the potential for positive change.

Troubleshooting: "I feel overwhelmed!" Break it down. Tackle challenges one step at a time. Each small victory contributes to the overall triumph. It's like navigating a maze; you don't need to see the entire path, just the next step.

Step 2: Cultivating Adaptability

In the garden of resilience, adaptability is the seed that ensures continuous growth. Life is dynamic, and being able to adjust your sails in the face of storms is a key resilience-building technique. It's like having a repertoire of dance moves, adapting to the rhythm of life's changes.

Troubleshooting: "I fear change!" Start small. Embrace minor changes and gradually work your way up. It's a gradual dance with adaptability, allowing you to build confidence in facing larger shifts.

Step 3: Building a Supportive Network

Resilience is not a solo endeavor; it's a team sport. Cultivate positive relationships and surround yourself with a supportive network. Having allies during tough times provides strength and perspective. It's like having teammates cheering you on in the game of life.

Troubleshooting: "I tend to isolate myself!" Reach out. Share your challenges with someone you trust. Positive connections serve as anchors during storms, providing stability and reassurance.

Step 4: Practicing Self-Compassion

Resilience begins with self-compassion, the gentle acknowledgment that setbacks are part of the human experience. Treat yourself with the kindness you would offer a friend facing challenges. It's like becoming your own compassionate coach, encouraging yourself through difficulties.

Troubleshooting: "I'm too hard on myself!" Challenge negative self-talk. Replace self-criticism with supportive and encouraging language. You are your greatest ally, and self-compassion is the armor that shields you from harsh judgments.

Step 5: Developing Problem-Solving Skills

Resilience involves navigating challenges with a strategic mindset. Instead of viewing problems as roadblocks, see them as puzzles to be solved. Cultivate problem-solving skills, breaking challenges into manageable steps. It's like having a toolkit equipped with problem-solving gadgets.

Troubleshooting: "I feel stuck!" Seek guidance. Consult with mentors, friends, or professionals. Sometimes an outside perspective provides new insights and solutions. It's like having a co-pilot during moments of turbulence.

Key Takeaways:

- Resilience is cultivated through a positive perspective.
- Adaptability is the key to navigating life's changes.
- Building a supportive network enhances resilience.
- Practicing self-compassion is foundational for resilience.
- Developing problem-solving skills empowers resilience.

Next Steps:

Ready to strengthen your resilience muscle? Pick one technique that resonates with you and start incorporating it into your daily life. Overcoming challenges is not about avoiding them but about building the skills to navigate and emerge stronger from them. Onward to resilience!

Learning from Setbacks

Greetings, life adventurers! In this exploration, we'll embark on the enlightening journey of learning from setbacks, transforming each stumble into a stepping stone for personal growth and resilience. Imagine setbacks as not roadblocks but as signposts guiding you toward invaluable lessons and newfound strength.

Step 1: Embrace the Lesson Within

Setbacks are not failures; they are life's curriculum. Embrace the mindset that each setback carries a lesson within it. It's like uncovering hidden treasures in the midst of challenges, gaining wisdom that propels you forward.

Troubleshooting: "I can't see the lesson!" Reflect on the experience. What happened, and how did it make you feel? Sometimes, the lesson is revealed through self-reflection, providing insights for future endeavors.

Step 2: Shift Your Perspective

Imagine setbacks as a change in scenery, an opportunity to view your journey from a different angle. Shift your perspective from seeing setbacks as obstacles to perceiving them as detours leading to unexpected discoveries. It's like taking a scenic route that offers unexpected beauty.

Troubleshooting: "I feel stuck!" Change your vantage point. Seek advice from others, read about similar experiences, or engage in activities that broaden your perspective. A shift in view often unveils new possibilities.

Step 3: Extract Tangible Insights

Setbacks are rich soil for cultivating tangible insights. Analyze the situation objectively. What worked, what didn't, and why? It's like distilling lessons from the experience, creating a roadmap for future endeavors.

Troubleshooting: "I'm overwhelmed!" Break it down. Focus on one aspect at a time. What can you learn from the specific challenges you faced? It's like solving a puzzle, each piece contributes to the bigger picture.

Step 4: Adjust Your Approach

Learning from setbacks is not just about understanding; it's about adapting. Consider how you can adjust your approach based on the insights gained. It's like refining your strategy, turning setbacks into catalysts for personal and professional evolution.

Troubleshooting: "I'm afraid of making the same mistakes!" Iterate. Implement small changes and observe their impact. Adjustments don't have to be drastic; even subtle shifts can lead to significant improvements.

Step 5: Cultivate Resilience

Setbacks are the raw material for resilience. Cultivate resilience by viewing challenges as opportunities to build inner strength. It's like forging a steel blade – each setback tempers your resilience, making you more robust and resilient in the face of future challenges.

Troubleshooting: "I feel defeated!" Reframe the narrative. Instead of focusing on the setback itself, concentrate on the growth it catalyzed. You are not defined by the setback but by your response to it.

Key Takeaways:

- Setbacks are not failures but opportunities for growth.
- Shift your perspective to uncover hidden lessons.
- Extract tangible insights to create a roadmap for the future.
- Adjust your approach based on the lessons learned.
- Cultivate resilience as a byproduct of setbacks.

Next Steps:

Ready to transform setbacks into springboards for growth? Choose one setback you've encountered recently, and apply these steps. As you embrace the lessons within setbacks, you'll find yourself not just bouncing back but leaping forward toward a more resilient and wiser version of yourself.

Developing Coping Strategies

Greetings, resilience architects! In this chapter, we'll delve into the art of developing coping strategies, your toolkit for navigating the inevitable ups and downs of life. Think of coping strategies as your trusty companions, ready to lend a hand when challenges arise. Let's explore the steps to build a robust set of coping skills.

Step 1: Identify Stressors and Triggers
Understanding your stressors and triggers is the first step in crafting effective coping strategies. What situations or events tend to heighten your stress levels? By identifying these, you gain insight into the specific challenges you need to address.

Troubleshooting: "I'm not sure what triggers me!" Keep a stress journal. Note down situations, emotions, and reactions. Patterns may emerge, revealing the root causes of your stress.

Step 2: Explore Healthy Outlets for Expression
Coping strategies are like release valves for built-up pressure. Explore healthy outlets for expressing your emotions, be it through journaling, art, music, or physical activity. It's like giving your emotions a constructive channel to flow.

Troubleshooting: "I'm not creative!" Experiment. You don't need to be an artist. Engage in activities that feel natural to you, whether it's a brisk walk, a heartfelt journal entry, or playing your favorite instrument.

Step 3: Practice Mindfulness and Relaxation Techniques

Mindfulness and relaxation techniques are anchors in stormy seas. Incorporate practices like deep breathing, meditation, or progressive muscle relaxation into your daily routine. They serve as grounding mechanisms, helping you stay centered in the midst of chaos.

Troubleshooting: "I can't find time to relax!" Start small. Dedicate a few minutes each day to a mindfulness practice. It could be as brief as focusing on your breath during a break or practicing a quick body scan before bed.

Step 4: Build a Support Network

Your support network is a key component of your coping arsenal. Cultivate relationships with friends, family, or support groups. Having someone to share your thoughts and feelings with provides both emotional validation and practical support.

Troubleshooting: "I'm not comfortable sharing!" Start with a trusted friend or family member. It's about building trust gradually. As you experience the benefits of sharing, you may feel more comfortable expanding your support network.

Step 5: Establish Healthy Lifestyle Habits

Physical well-being is intertwined with mental well-being. Adopting healthy lifestyle habits, such as regular exercise, a balanced diet, and sufficient sleep, enhances your overall resilience. It's like fortifying the foundation from which you face life's challenges.

Troubleshooting: "I don't have time for self-care!" Prioritize. Small adjustments, like a 15-minute workout or choosing nutritious snacks, can have a big impact. Recognize self-care as an investment in your long-term well-being.

Step 6: Develop Problem-Solving Skills

Coping is not just about managing emotions; it's about addressing the root causes of stress. Sharpen your problem-solving skills, breaking challenges into manageable steps. It's like becoming a proactive navigator, steering through difficulties with strategic finesse.

Troubleshooting: "I get overwhelmed with big problems!" Break them down. Focus on one aspect at a time. Problem-solving is incremental. Each solved component contributes to resolving the larger issue.

Key Takeaways:
- Identify stressors and triggers for targeted coping.
- Explore healthy outlets for expressing emotions.
- Practice mindfulness and relaxation techniques.
- Build a supportive network for emotional validation.
- Establish healthy lifestyle habits for overall resilience.
- Develop problem-solving skills for proactive coping.

Next Steps:

Ready to enrich your coping toolkit? Select one or two strategies that resonate with you and integrate them into your routine. Remember, developing coping skills is an ongoing process. As you experiment with different techniques, you'll discover the personalized combination that empowers you to navigate life's challenges with resilience and grace.

Chapter 7

Lifestyle Changes for Long-Term Mental Wellness

Sleep and its Impact on Mood

In this pivotal chapter, we delve into the profound connection between sleep and mood. Think of sleep as the nocturnal architect shaping the foundation of your mental well-being. Let's explore how embracing healthy sleep habits can be a cornerstone in your journey toward enduring mental wellness.

Step 1: Understanding the Sleep-Mood Nexus
Imagine your sleep as the maestro orchestrating a symphony of emotions. The quality and duration of your sleep directly impact your mood. Understand the intricate dance between sleep and mood, recognizing that a well-rested night sets the stage for a brighter tomorrow.

Troubleshooting: "I don't see the connection!" Keep a sleep diary. Note your sleep patterns and mood upon waking. Over time, patterns may emerge, revealing the profound interplay between your nightly rest and daily emotional states.

Step 2: Prioritizing Consistent Sleep Patterns

Consistency is the melody that lulls your mind into restful slumber. Aim for a consistent sleep schedule, going to bed and waking up at the same time each day. It's like tuning your internal clock to a harmonious rhythm, promoting overall mental harmony.

Troubleshooting: "My schedule is unpredictable!" Establish a wind-down routine. Regardless of your schedule, create a pre-sleep ritual to signal to your body that it's time to unwind. This could include dimming lights, reading a book, or practicing relaxation exercises.

Step 3: Creating a Sleep-Conducive Environment

Your sleep environment is the canvas on which restful nights are painted. Make your bedroom a sanctuary for sleep by keeping it cool, dark, and quiet. It's like crafting a peaceful oasis, inviting tranquility and inviting restful slumber.

Troubleshooting: "I can't control external noise!" Invest in earplugs or use white noise machines to drown out disturbances. Consider blackout curtains to minimize external light. Small adjustments can significantly enhance your sleep environment.

Step 4: Limiting Stimulants and Screens

Imagine stimulants and screens as mischievous sprites disrupting the tranquility of your sleep kingdom. Limit caffeine and screen time, especially close to bedtime. It's like ushering out the rowdy party guests, ensuring a serene and undisturbed night.

Troubleshooting: "I can't function without coffee!" Gradually reduce stimulant intake. Experiment with herbal teas or warm milk as calming alternatives. Your body will adjust, and you'll experience the natural energy rhythm that comes with quality sleep.

Step 5: Engaging in Relaxation Techniques

Picture relaxation techniques as gentle lullabies calming your restless mind. Incorporate practices like deep breathing, meditation, or gentle stretches before bedtime. It's like a soothing bedtime story, easing your mind into a state of peaceful repose.

Troubleshooting: "My mind races at night!" Practice mindfulness. When intrusive thoughts emerge, gently guide your focus back to your breath or a calming visualization. It's a skill that improves with consistent practice.

Step 6: Seeking Professional Guidance

If sleep challenges persist, consider seeking guidance from a sleep specialist or mental health professional.

Persistent sleep issues might indicate underlying factors that a professional can help address. It's like consulting a sleep architect to optimize your nocturnal habitat.

Troubleshooting: "I've tried everything!" Consultation is not admission of defeat but a proactive step toward optimal well-being. Professionals can conduct assessments, provide personalized recommendations, and guide you toward restful nights.

Key Takeaways:
- Recognize the connection between sleep and mood.
- Prioritize consistent sleep patterns for harmony.
- Create a sleep-conducive environment in your bedroom.
- Limit stimulants and screens to promote tranquility.
- Engage in relaxation techniques for a peaceful transition to sleep.
- Seek professional guidance for persistent sleep challenges.

Next Steps:

Ready to embrace the transformative power of sleep on your mood? Choose one or two steps to incorporate into your nightly routine.

Managing Stress Effectively

Hello stress navigators! In this chapter, we'll embark on a journey to master the art of stress management – a crucial skill for maintaining mental well-being in the face of life's challenges. Imagine stress as the ebb and flow of a turbulent sea, and let's explore how to ride its waves with resilience and grace.

Step 1: Recognizing Stressors

Stress management begins with a keen awareness of the stressors in your life. Identify the sources that trigger stress, whether they are work-related, personal, or environmental. It's like creating a map of the stress landscape, allowing you to navigate with precision.

Troubleshooting: "I'm not sure what's stressing me!" Keep a stress journal. Record situations, feelings, and your reactions. Patterns may emerge, shedding light on the specific stressors you need to address.

Step 2: Developing a Stress Response Plan

Imagine stress management as a well-rehearsed dance, where each step is intentional and purposeful. Develop a stress response plan that includes healthy coping mechanisms. Whether it's deep breathing, a short walk, or a moment of mindfulness, having a go-to response helps you regain balance when stress knocks.

Troubleshooting: "I don't know what calms me!" Experiment. Try different stress-relief activities, and observe their impact. It could be listening to music, practicing yoga, or spending time in nature. Your personalized stress response plan is a dynamic tool that evolves with your discoveries.

Step 3: Prioritizing Self-Care

Self-care is the anchor that keeps you steady amidst life's storms. Prioritize activities that nurture your physical, mental, and emotional well-being. It's like tending to a garden – each act of self-care contributes to the overall vibrancy of your life.

Troubleshooting: "I feel guilty taking time for myself!" Reframe the narrative. Self-care is not selfish; it's a necessity. Recognize that taking care of yourself equips you to better handle life's challenges and support those around you.

Step 4: Time Management and Boundaries

Stress often creeps in when boundaries are blurred, and time slips away. Develop effective time management strategies and set boundaries that protect your well-being. It's like constructing a fortress, safeguarding your time and energy from unnecessary stressors.

Troubleshooting: "I struggle with saying no!" Practice assertiveness. Communicate your limits clearly and respectfully. Setting boundaries is a skill that improves with time and practice.

Step 5: Building a Support System

Your support system is a powerful stress-buster. Cultivate positive relationships with friends, family, or support groups. Sharing your thoughts and feelings provides not only emotional validation but also practical support in times of need.

Troubleshooting: "I'm hesitant to ask for help!" Start small. Reach out to someone you trust and share your thoughts. Vulnerability strengthens connections and reinforces your support system.

Step 6: Embracing Healthy Habits

A healthy lifestyle is a shield against stress. Incorporate regular exercise, a balanced diet, and sufficient sleep into your routine. These habits bolster your physical and mental resilience, enabling you to face stress with a fortified mindset.

Troubleshooting: "I'm too busy for healthy habits!" Prioritize. Small adjustments, like short bursts of exercise or choosing nutritious snacks, can have a significant impact. Recognize that these habits are investments in your long-term well-being.

Key Takeaways:
- Recognize and understand your stressors.
- Develop a personalized stress response plan.
- Prioritize self-care as a fundamental practice.
- Manage time effectively and set boundaries.
- Cultivate a supportive network.
- Embrace healthy habits for physical and mental resilience.

Next Steps:
Ready to master the art of stress management? Choose one or two steps that resonate with you and integrate them into your daily life. As you cultivate a personalized stress management toolkit, you'll discover the resilience and strength to navigate life's challenges with poise and vitality.

Balancing Work and Personal Life

Hello life jugglers! In this chapter, we're stepping into the delicate dance of balancing work and personal life – a high-stakes act that requires finesse, intention, and a dash of self-compassion. Imagine your life as a grand performance, and let's explore how to harmonize the various elements for a truly satisfying and well-balanced show.

Step 1: Define Your Priorities

Balancing work and personal life begins with clarity on your priorities. What matters most to you? Identify your core values and the aspects of work and personal life that align with them. It's like setting the stage with the elements that truly resonate with your heart.

Troubleshooting: "Everything feels important!" Prioritize. Not everything can be a top priority. Identify the non-negotiables and the aspects that can flex based on the demands of the moment.

Step 2: Set Boundaries

Boundaries are the spotlight that keeps each part of your life from stealing the show at the wrong time. Establish clear boundaries between work and personal life. Define specific times for work, leisure, and personal commitments. It's like choreographing the movements of a well-coordinated dance.

Troubleshooting: "I feel guilty setting boundaries!" Revisit your priorities. Boundaries are not about neglecting one aspect for another but about ensuring that each gets the attention it deserves. Communicate your boundaries respectfully and assertively.

Step 3: Master Time Management

Time management is the rhythm that guides the tempo of your daily routine. Develop effective time management strategies to optimize your productivity at work and create dedicated time for personal pursuits. It's like composing a symphony where each note has its designated moment.

Troubleshooting: "I'm overwhelmed with tasks!" Break it down. Prioritize tasks based on urgency and importance. Delegate when possible, and don't hesitate to ask for support.

Step 4: Schedule Quality Personal Time

Your personal time is the intermission that rejuvenates your spirit. Schedule regular moments for self-care, hobbies, and quality time with loved ones. It's like ensuring there are vibrant interludes in the play of your life.

Troubleshooting: "I never have time for myself!" Make it non-negotiable. Just as you prioritize work meetings, prioritize personal time. Whether it's reading a book, going for a walk, or enjoying a hobby, these moments contribute significantly to your overall well-being.

Step 5: Learn to Say No

Saying no is the director's cut, ensuring that your life's narrative aligns with your vision. It's okay to decline additional work tasks or social invitations when it interferes with your established balance. It's like editing scenes that don't serve the plot.

Troubleshooting: "I fear disappointing others!" Practice assertiveness. Communicate your limitations respectfully and be clear about what you can commit to. Remember, saying no is a skill that strengthens with practice.

Step 6: Foster Open Communication

Communication is the dialogue that maintains harmony between work and personal life. Foster open communication with your colleagues, superiors, and loved ones about your priorities and challenges. It's like ensuring everyone in the cast is on the same page for a successful performance.

Troubleshooting: "I'm afraid my colleagues won't understand!" Be transparent. Most people appreciate honesty. Communicate your needs and boundaries, and you might be surprised by the support and understanding you receive.

Key Takeaways:
- Define your priorities and align them with your values.
- Set clear boundaries between work and personal life.
- Master time management to optimize productivity.
- Schedule regular, quality personal time.
- Learn to say no when necessary.
- Foster open communication with colleagues and loved ones.

Next Steps:
Ready to bring balance to the stage of your life? Choose one or two steps that resonate with you and integrate them into your routine. As you refine the art of balancing work and personal life, you'll find yourself not just navigating the dual roles but orchestrating a symphony where each element harmonizes for a fulfilling and well-rounded life performance.

Chapter 8

Celebrating Progress and Maintaining Well-being

Recognizing Achievements

Greetings, champions of well-being! In this celebratory chapter, we're going to focus on the art of recognizing achievements, a key ingredient in the recipe for sustained mental wellness. Picture this as the standing ovation for your life's performance, where each achievement, big or small, deserves its moment in the spotlight.

Step 1: Embrace the Power of Acknowledgment
Acknowledgment is the applause that fuels your journey. Take a moment to acknowledge and celebrate your achievements, no matter how modest. It's like giving yourself a well-deserved pat on the back, affirming the progress you've made.

Troubleshooting: "I downplay my achievements!" Practice self-compassion. Treat yourself as you would a friend. Recognize that every step forward is a triumph, and you deserve to revel in it.

Step 2: Cultivate a Success Journal

A success journal is the scrapbook of your victories, both big and small. Regularly document your achievements, reflecting on the challenges overcome and the growth experienced. It's like curating a gallery of your triumphs, providing a tangible reminder of your resilience.

Troubleshooting: "I forget my achievements!" Make it a habit. Set aside time regularly to jot down your successes. It could be daily, weekly, or even monthly. Consistency turns this into a powerful tool for maintaining a positive perspective.

Step 3: Share and Celebrate with Others

Sharing achievements is the joyous chorus that amplifies the melody of success. Don't hesitate to share your accomplishments with friends, family, or colleagues. Celebrate together and let their enthusiasm amplify your sense of achievement.

Troubleshooting: "I fear others will think I'm boasting!" Share with humility. Communicate your achievements in a genuine and humble manner. True friends and supporters will appreciate your wins.

Step 4: Set Milestones and Celebrate Progress

Milestones are the signposts that mark your journey. Set achievable milestones, and when you reach them, take a moment to celebrate. It's like breaking the journey into chapters, each deserving its own acknowledgment.

Troubleshooting: "I focus only on the end goal!" Break it down. Celebrate progress at various stages, not just the final destination. Recognize the effort you put into each phase of your journey.

Step 5: Reflect on Personal Growth

Personal growth is the ever-evolving narrative of your life. Take time to reflect on the lessons learned, skills acquired, and the person you've become. It's like standing back to admire the artwork of your personal development.

Troubleshooting: "I don't see the growth!" Journal your reflections. Write about the challenges you've faced and how you've overcome them. You'll likely discover a narrative of resilience and strength.

Step 6: Establish Rituals of Celebration

Rituals of celebration are the festive traditions that make achievements memorable. Establish personal rituals to celebrate your successes, it could be a special meal, a leisure activity, or a moment of quiet reflection. It's like creating your own joyous traditions.

Troubleshooting: "I forget to celebrate!" Set reminders. Make celebrating achievements a non-negotiable part of your journey. Set calendar alerts or tie celebrations to specific milestones to ensure they don't go unnoticed.

Key Takeaways:
- Embrace acknowledgment as a powerful tool.
- Cultivate a success journal to document achievements.
- Share and celebrate achievements with others.
- Set milestones and celebrate progress.
- Reflect on personal growth and lessons learned.
- Establish rituals of celebration for memorable moments.

Next Steps:
Ready to unleash the confetti for your achievements? Choose one or two steps that resonate with you and weave them into your routine. As you consistently recognize and celebrate your achievements, you'll infuse your life with a sense of accomplishment, resilience, and an enduring commitment to well-being.

Building Sustainable Habits

Hello habit architects! In this chapter, we're diving into the art of building sustainable habits – the cornerstone of lasting well-being. Think of habits as the architects of your daily life, shaping the structure of your routines and influencing your overall mental and physical health. Let's explore how to construct habits that endure the test of time.

Step 1: Start Small and Consistent

Small changes are the building blocks of enduring habits. Begin with tiny, manageable adjustments to your routine. It's like laying the foundation for a sturdy structure – start with a solid base, and it becomes easier to build upon.

Troubleshooting: "I want big changes!" Think micro. Break down your desired habit into the smallest possible action. Consistency in these small actions creates a powerful ripple effect over time.

Step 2: Anchor to Existing Habits

Anchor your new habit to an established routine. Associate the new behavior with something you already do consistently. It's like seamlessly blending the new into the familiar, making it more likely to stick.

Troubleshooting: "I forget to do it!" Pair your new habit with a specific trigger. For example, if you want to establish a morning stretching routine, link it to brushing your teeth. The association helps solidify the habit.

Step 3: Set Clear Triggers
Triggers are the catalysts that initiate your habits. Clearly define what triggers your habit. It's like creating a roadmap for your brain, signaling when it's time to engage in the desired behavior.

Troubleshooting: "I can't remember to do it!" Use cues like alarms, post-it notes, or smartphone reminders to prompt your habit. Consistent triggers create a natural inclination to perform the behavior.

Step 4: Gradual Progress and Patience
Building habits is a marathon, not a sprint. Gradually increase the intensity or duration of your habit over time. Patience is the scaffolding that supports the construction of lasting habits.

Troubleshooting: "I get discouraged!" Celebrate small wins. Acknowledge and celebrate each milestone, no matter how minor. It reinforces the habit loop and boosts motivation.

Step 5: Accountability and Support

Accountability is the sturdy beam that fortifies your habit structure. Share your habit goals with a friend or join a community where you can provide and receive support. It's like having a team of builders to keep you on track.

Troubleshooting: "I feel alone in this!" Seek a habit buddy or use apps that provide accountability. Knowing that someone else is aware of your goals can be a powerful motivator.

Step 6: Learn from Setbacks

Setbacks are the renovation opportunities in your habit-building journey. Instead of viewing them as failures, extract lessons from setbacks. It's like refining the blueprint of your habit, making it more resilient.

Troubleshooting: "I fall off the wagon!" Reflect on what led to the setback without self-judgment. Adjust your strategy and move forward. Each setback is a chance to refine and reinforce your habit-building approach.

Key Takeaways:
- Start with small, consistent changes.
- Anchor new habits to existing routines.
- Set clear triggers for your habits.

- Progress gradually and practice patience.
- Establish accountability and seek support.
- Learn from setbacks to refine your approach.

Next Steps:
Ready to build habits that stand the test of time? Choose one or two steps that resonate with you and incorporate them into your habit-building journey. As you construct and reinforce your habits, you'll be crafting a lifestyle that contributes to your well-being and long-term success.

Embracing a Lifelong Journey of Mental Wellness

Greetings, fellow travelers on the path of well-being! In this concluding chapter, we're venturing into the heart of embracing a lifelong journey of mental wellness. Consider this journey as a dynamic tapestry, woven with resilience, self-discovery, and a commitment to nurturing your mental health throughout the twists and turns of life.

Step 1: Embrace the Fluidity of Well-being
Well-being is not a fixed destination but a fluid journey. Embrace the ebb and flow of life, recognizing that your mental health may fluctuate. It's like navigating the currents of a river, sometimes calm, sometimes turbulent, but always in motion.

Reflection: "Am I failing if I struggle?" No, you're evolving. Challenges are not setbacks but opportunities for growth. Embrace the process, and be kind to yourself during both highs and lows.

Step 2: Cultivate a Growth Mindset
A growth mindset is the compass that guides you toward continuous improvement. View challenges as opportunities to learn and grow. It's like seeing each

obstacle as a stepping stone on the path to becoming the best version of yourself.

Reflection: "Can I change and grow?" Absolutely. Your mind is adaptable, capable of learning and evolving throughout your life. Embrace challenges as invitations for personal and mental growth.

Step 3: Prioritize Self-Compassion

Self-compassion is the gentle breeze that soothes your journey. Treat yourself with the same kindness and understanding you would offer to a friend. It's like offering a comforting hand to yourself during moments of struggle.

Reflection: "Do I deserve self-compassion?" Yes, you do. Recognize that imperfections are part of being human. Embracing self-compassion doesn't mean perfection; it means acknowledging your humanity with warmth.

Step 4: Build and Maintain Supportive Connections

Supportive connections are the sturdy bridges that make the journey more manageable. Cultivate and nurture relationships with those who uplift and support you. It's like having fellow travelers to share the joys and burdens of the road.

Reflection: "Can relationships impact my mental wellness?" Absolutely. Positive connections provide emotional nourishment and resilience. Surround yourself with those who encourage your well-being.

Step 5: Continuously Learn and Adapt

Learning and adaptation are the navigation tools in your mental wellness toolkit. Stay curious, seek knowledge, and be open to adapting your strategies as needed. It's like upgrading your map as you discover new terrain.

Reflection: "Can I keep evolving?" Indeed. Your understanding of mental wellness may evolve over time. Stay open to new insights, therapies, and practices that align with your evolving self.

Step 6: Celebrate Milestones, Big and Small

Milestones are the celebratory markers along your journey. Acknowledge and celebrate your progress, no matter how incremental. It's like pausing to appreciate the scenery as you reach each summit.

Reflection: "Should I celebrate even small victories?" Absolutely. Small victories contribute to significant progress. Celebrate them as evidence of your resilience and determination.

Key Takeaways:

- Embrace the fluid nature of mental well-being.
- Cultivate a growth mindset for continuous improvement.
- Prioritize self-compassion in moments of struggle.
- Build and maintain supportive connections.
- Continuously learn and adapt your strategies.
- Celebrate milestones, big and small.

Final Reflection:

As you stand at the intersection of your past, present, and future, remember that mental wellness is a lifelong journey. Embrace it with the same enthusiasm you would a grand adventure, knowing that each step contributes to the narrative of a resilient, thriving, and ever-evolving you. May your journey be rich with self-discovery, compassion, and a deep sense of well-being. Safe travels!

Conclusion

Dear fellow explorers of well-being,

As we reach the final pages of our guide, "How to Overcome Depression Through Diet, Exercise, and Mindset Shifts: A Holistic Guide to Improving Your Mood and Mental Health," it's not just the end of a book; it's the beginning of a transformative journey. Together, we've ventured through the realms of the mind and body, uncovering the intricacies of mental wellness.

In embracing the fluidity of well-being, we've acknowledged that this journey is not a one-time expedition but a lifelong sojourn. Our mindset, like a compass, directs us towards growth, while self-compassion serves as a comforting companion during moments of challenge.

We've constructed habits, much like architects designing the blueprint of a fulfilling life. From the foundation of small, consistent changes to the scaffolding of accountability, each habit becomes a sturdy pillar supporting your mental health.

Through the chapters, you've cultivated supportive connections, recognizing the importance of fellow travelers on this path. As you continuously learn and adapt, your toolkit for mental wellness expands, ensuring you're well-equipped for the twists and turns ahead.

And now, as we stand at this juncture, it's time to celebrate. Celebrate the progress made, the milestones reached, and the resilience demonstrated. Each achievement, whether big or small, is a testament to your dedication to well-being.

So, here's to you – the intrepid reader who embarked on this holistic journey. May you carry the wisdom gained within these pages as a lantern guiding you through the complexities of life. The title of this book is not just a guide; it's an invitation to embrace a life rich in self-discovery, compassion, and continuous well-being.

As the final chapter closes, remember that your journey is ongoing, and the narrative of your mental wellness is a story written with every step you take. May your path be filled with moments of joy, growth, and a profound sense of fulfillment.

Safe travels on your lifelong journey of mental wellness.

With warm regards,

www.ingramcontent.com/pod-product-compliance
Lightning Source LLC
Chambersburg PA
CBHW060947260726
48661CB00005B/1786